HUMAN ANATOMY FOR KIDS

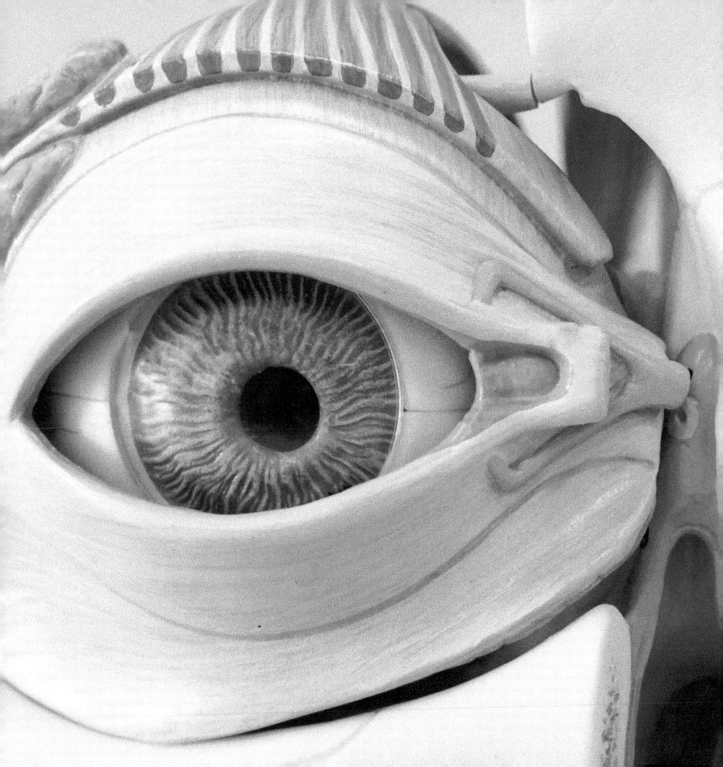

HUMAN ANATOMY
FOR KIDS

A JUNIOR SCIENTIST'S GUIDE
to How We Move, Breathe, and Grow

KRISTIE WAGNER

**ROCKRIDGE
PRESS**

For my son—may you never stop learning!

For general information on our other products and services or to obtain technical support, please contact our Customer Care Department within the United States at (866) 744-2665, or outside the United States at (510) 253-0500.

Rockridge Press publishes its books in a variety of electronic and print formats. Some content that appears in print may not be available in electronic books, and vice versa.

Series Designer: Junior Scientist Design Team
Interior and Cover Designer: John Calmeyer
Art Producer: Sara Feinstein
Editor: Erum Khan
Production Editor: Ruth Sakata Corley
Production Manager: Holly Haydash

Illustrations © 2021 Conor Buckley. Photography used under license from Shutterstock.com and iStock.com.

ISBN: Print 978-1-64876-863-7
eBook 978-1-64876-260-4
R0

CONTENTS

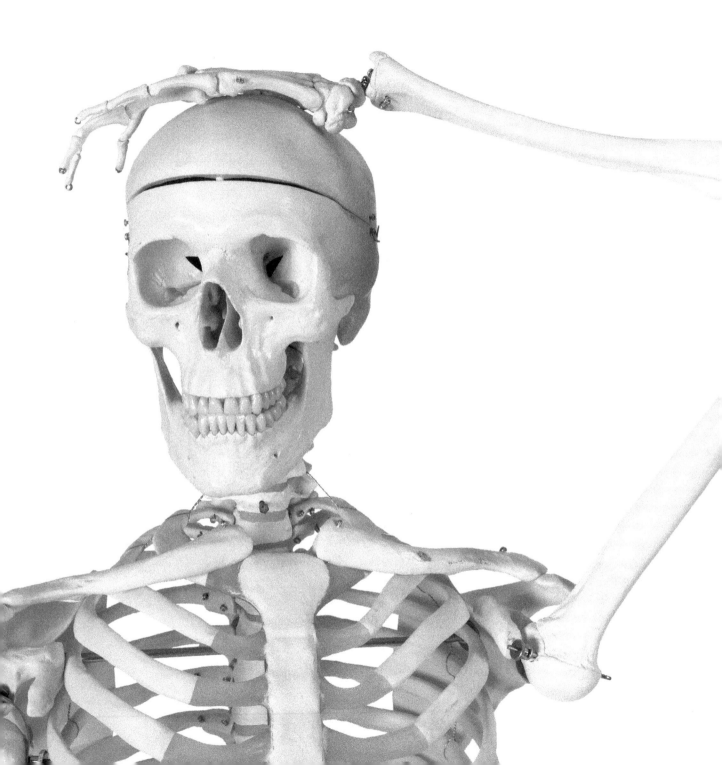

WELCOME, JUNIOR SCIENTIST!

Are you curious about what your body looks like under your skin? Do you wonder where your food goes after you eat it? Why you sweat? Or how your body protects you from germs? You are about to find out! This book is a handy guide to human **anatomy**—which is another word for all your body's parts.

Human bodies are made of different **cells**, **tissues**, and **organs**. They all work together to keep your body healthy, growing, and moving. They make you *you*. In this book, you will take a look at each of those parts and learn how they help you move, think, and grow.

This book has seven chapters that will take you on a tour of your body. After learning some body basics, you'll read about how your body defends itself against germs, how it moves, thinks, breathes, turns food into energy, and creates new humans. Does this sound cool to you? Then, let's get started!

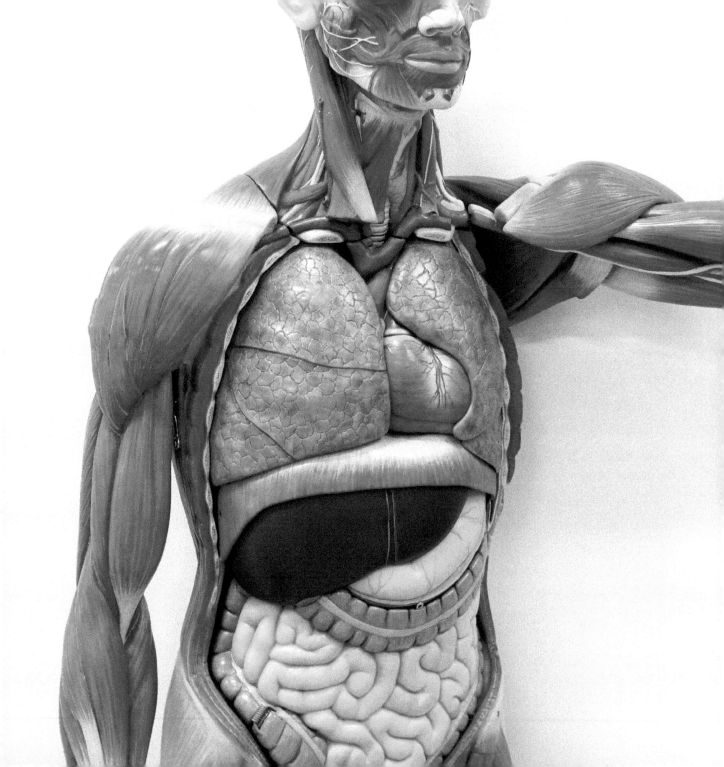

CHAPTER ONE

THE HUMAN BODY

The human body is like an amazing machine. It is made up of many different parts that do very different jobs to keep you alive and healthy. All those many parts work in groups called systems. Each system has its own special job to do.

Human cells, tissues, organs, and organ systems all work together to keep your body in **homeostasis**. Homeostasis means that your body is in balance and working the best it can. It stays this way no matter what is going on outside the body. Everything is connected, so if one part doesn't do its job, the others have trouble doing theirs. From the tiniest cell to the biggest system, they are all important.

What Is a Body?

Every living thing, or organism, has a body. Animals, plants, and even organisms like bacteria all have bodies! Animal bodies (like ours) are made up of a lot of different parts, from tiny ones you need a microscope to see, to larger ones you look at every day in the mirror. They all work together to build *you*!

Animal bodies are all made up of different kinds of tiny cells. These cells fit together to build tissues. Tissues fit together to build organs and organ systems. Each organ system does a specific job in your body, like breathing or digesting food. All organ systems work together as one to keep you happy and healthy.

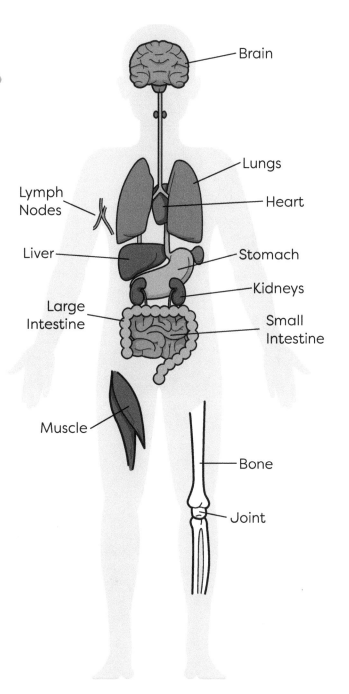

Cells

Cells are the smallest parts of every living thing. Everything in a body is made of cells. This is why cells are called the building blocks of life.

Humans have many different types of cells. What do they each do?

- **Blood cells** bring oxygen and nutrients to every single cell in your body.

- **Bone cells** make your bones grow and make blood cells.

- **Brain cells** send messages to all the different body systems.

- **Egg and sperm cells** help make new humans!

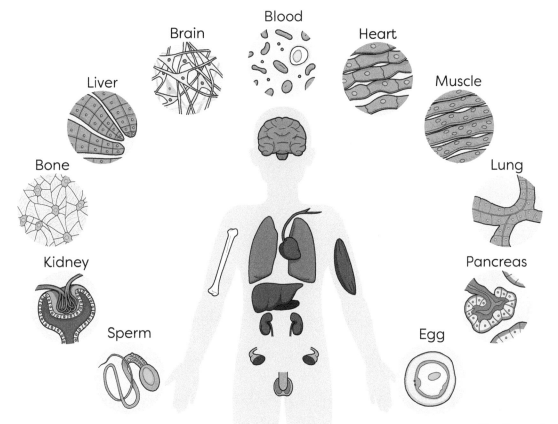

Brain

Blood

Heart

Liver

Muscle

Bone

Lung

Kidney

Pancreas

Sperm

Egg

- **Liver and kidney cells** remove **toxins**, or waste, from your blood.

- **Lung cells** take oxygen out of the air you breathe.

- **Muscle cells** let you move.

- **Pancreatic cells (cells in the pancreas)** help you digest food.

When similar cells group together, they form tissues.

Tissues

Tissues aren't just something you blow your nose in! Tissues in your body are made up of cells that share the same job. Your body has four main types of tissue: **connective tissue**, epithelial tissue, muscle tissue, and nerve tissue.

- **Connective tissues** do just what they say—they connect different parts of your body to one another. They can also insulate you to keep you warm.

- **Epithelial tissue** is part of the skin, and it helps protect your body by covering it. It keeps harmful things from getting inside your body. It can also get rid of waste in the form of sweat.

- **Muscle tissues** contract, or bunch up, and relax to move parts of the body.

- **Nerve tissues** control *how* your body moves. They also help you sense, remember, feel emotions, and solve problems.

Connective Tissue

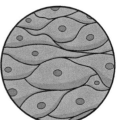
Epithelial Tissue

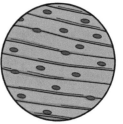
Muscle Tissue

Nerve Tissue

When groups of similar tissues work together, they form organs.

What Are Organs?

Organs are made up of tissues working together to do a special job. Each organ does something different and important for your body. The brain, stomach, skin, lungs, and heart are all organs—and there are many more!

Groups of organs and tissues come together to form **organ systems**. For example, the muscular system has three different types of **muscles** that work together to help you move your body. Alone, the different muscles wouldn't be able to do their jobs, but together they make an awesome team!

Organs Working Together

How many organ systems are inside your body right now? 12! Put them all together and you have a working human body.

Each system has a different job. We'll discuss each job in more detail later in the book.

IT'S ALL ABOUT CHEMISTRY

Did you know that your body is made of about 60 chemicals? Some are in large amounts and some are in tiny amounts. There are six main chemicals that make up most of you: oxygen, carbon, hydrogen, nitrogen, calcium, and phosphorus. More than half of you is made up of oxygen!

Liver

Thyroid

Lungs

Thymus

Stomach

Kidney

Male
Reproductive
System

Urinary
System

Pancreas

Intestines

Female
Reproductive
System

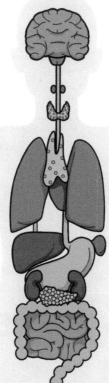

ORGAN SYSTEM	MAJOR ORGANS AND TISSUES	MAIN JOB
Integumentary	Skin, hair, nails	Protects the body and maintains homeostasis
Immune	Bone marrow, spleen	Defends against germs
Lymphatic	Lymph nodes, lymph vessels	Defends against germs
Skeletal	Bones, cartilage, joints	Gives the body shape and support
Muscular	Cardiac muscle, skeletal muscle, smooth muscle	Lets the body move
Nervous	Brain, spinal cord, nerves	Makes sense of your surroundings
Circulatory	Heart, blood vessels	Delivers oxygen and nutrients
Respiratory	Lungs, trachea, larynx	Takes in oxygen by breathing
Digestive	Stomach, liver, intestines	Digests food for the body to use
Urinary	Kidneys, bladder	Removes waste from the blood
Endocrine	Pituitary gland, hypothalamus, pancreas, adrenal glands	Makes hormones
Reproductive	Ovaries, testes	Makes hormones and cells for reproduction

HOMEOSTASIS: THE BODY IN BALANCE

Your body's systems all talk to one another to maintain homeostasis. That means everything in your body is at just the right level. One example of this is your body temperature. Unless your body is fighting germs, your temperature is always around 98.6 degrees Fahrenheit—even if it's freezing cold outside!

If you are outside and the Sun is shining, you may begin to feel hot. Your skin sends a message to your brain telling it that things are getting a little too steamy. The brain sends a message back to your skin, directing it to sweat. When you sweat, you cool down. This keeps your body in homeostasis. If your body got too hot, your cells wouldn't be able to do their jobs. (They also wouldn't be able to do their jobs if your body got too cold.)

Your body can also take itself out of homeostasis on purpose. For example, your brain might raise your temperature to fight germs that are inside your body. When your body is under attack, it is important to get rid of the cause as quickly as possible. As soon as the danger is gone, your brain brings your body back to homeostasis.

DISCOVERING DNA

All living things need instructions in order to move and grow. Inside every cell in your body is a chain we call **DNA**. DNA contains all the instructions your cells need to make you who you are. Let's look at some strawberry DNA at home! *(Ask an adult to help you set up and clean up.)*

What You Need:

FROZEN STRAWBERRY
RESEALABLE BAG
TEASPOON
3 OR 4 TEASPOONS OF DISH SOAP
COFFEE FILTER
CLEAR CUP
RUBBER BAND
2 TEASPOONS OF RUBBING ALCOHOL (THAT HAS BEEN IN THE FREEZER)
TWEEZERS

1. Put a frozen strawberry in a resealable bag. Seal it and squish the strawberry until it has no large pieces left. Add 3 or 4 teaspoons of dish soap to the bag.

2. Put a coffee filter in a cup and hold it in place with a rubber band around the top. Pour the contents of the bag into the coffee filter. Wait 5 to 10 minutes. Remove the coffee filter.

3. Add 2 teaspoons of rubbing alcohol to the solution in the cup.

4. Use the tweezers to gently grab the DNA from the surface of the solution. (It looks like SNOT!) Observe and enjoy!

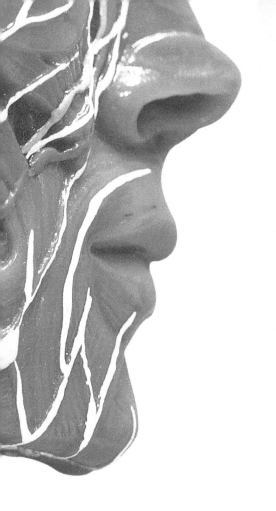

CHAPTER TWO

YOUR BODY'S DEFENSE SYSTEMS

Every day, your body comes into contact with **pathogens**, or germs, that can make you sick. Luckily, your body has several ways to defend you from those pathogens. Your skin is your body's first line of defense. Your skin, hair, and nails are called the integumentary (in-teg-you-men-ta-ree) system. If germs manage to get past your integumentary system, your immune system and lymphatic system spring into action to fight germs and protect you from future invasions! Let's dive in and learn more about how your body's defense systems work.

The Skin You're In

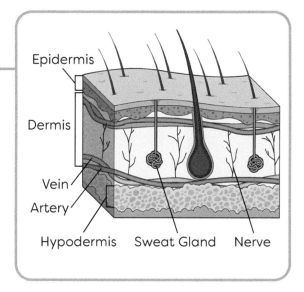

Epidermis
Dermis
Vein
Artery
Hypodermis   Sweat Gland   Nerve

Your skin is your largest organ. It covers your entire body and keeps many harmful germs out. It's made up of three layers.

The layer of skin you see is called the epidermis. Just under that is a layer called the dermis. This is where you will find sweat **glands** (where you sweat), **blood vessels** (where blood flows), hair follicles (where hair grows from), and nerve endings (which help your skin feel things). Under your dermis is fat, which helps control your body temperature.

Your skin also has special cells called sensory receptors. They team up with nerve endings to send information to your brain. When you touch something, the sensory receptors tell your brain that it feels smooth or rough. You can also sense temperature and respond to it. You will sweat when you're warm to cool off and shiver when you are cold to warm up.

FRECKLES

Freckles form when some skin cells make extra color pigment, called melanin (mel-uh-nin). Freckles are very common in people who have light skin and red or blond hair, but they can also be caused by the Sun's ultraviolet (or UV) radiation. People may get freckles when they get older. That's because skin makes more melanin as a person ages.

Your thinnest skin is on your eyelids, and your thickest skin is on the heels of your feet. The skin on the palms of your hands and soles of your feet doesn't grow hair! This skin is called glabrous (glay-brus) skin.

Hair

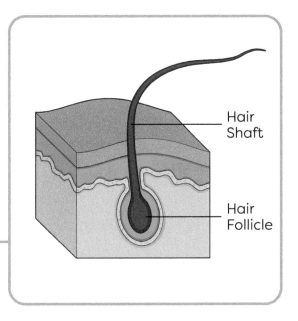

Hair does a lot more than just look nice. It protects your body—even inside your nose and ears! Hair is made of a protein called keratin. Each strand of hair grows out of a follicle. This is a special tunnel-shaped area in your skin.

There are two types of hair: vellus and terminal. Vellus hair is short and thin. You have vellus hair all over your body. Some people call it peach fuzz. Terminal hair is longer, thicker, and easier to see on the body. You have terminal hair on your head. Adults also have it on their faces (beards), under their arms, and other places. Hair grows the fastest when you are young and slows down after about age 30.

Nails

Your nails are also made of keratin. They help protect the soft ends of your fingers and toes.

Nails grow from a root called the nail bed. There are blood vessels under the nail bed, which is why your nails look red or pink. As the nail grows, it comes out of the cuticle (kyoo-ti-cal). This is where the skin and nail meet. The cuticle protects the nail as it grows. New nail cells replace old nail cells and push them along the nail bed. The old cells flatten and get harder. They become your fingernails! Fingernails grow very slowly. It can take three to six months to replace a nail you've lost.

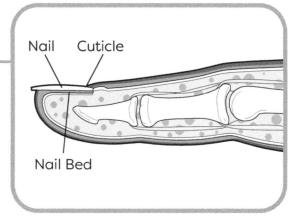

Nail   Cuticle

Nail Bed

AHHH . . . CHOO!

A sneeze is one of the ways your body gets rid of things that don't belong there. When you feel a tickle in your nose, your body prepares to sneeze. You breathe in quickly, close your eyes, and a muscle underneath your ribs pushes the air—and dust or germs—out super fast. Some people sneeze when they look at bright light or the Sun. This is called photic (fo-tik) sneezing.

Fighting Off Sickness

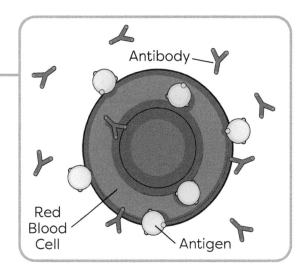

Your skin does a good job of keeping germs out. But what happens when germs get in? That's when your immune system comes to the rescue! Your immune system has two ways of handling things.

First, your body has something called an **innate response**. It works quickly and targets anything and everything that is a threat to the body. It attacks everything the same way. Your skin, mucus (boogers!), and defense cells all are part of this response. Special cells called white blood cells patrol the body and gobble up any pathogens they find.

Your body is also able to target specific pathogens. This is called an **adaptive response**. It kicks in when the innate response can't get rid of the germ by itself. White blood cells create **antibodies** for the pathogen. These are proteins that fight the pathogen—they

also remember how to fight it in case that pathogen comes back in the future. This is how you get **immunity** to a sickness. Immunity is your ability to fight off germs without medicine.

LYMPHOCYTES TO THE RESCUE!

The lymphatic system also fights germs. Lymph (limf) nodes are part of this system. They are basically little bean-shaped filters that remove harmful things from your blood. **Lymph nodes** are found all over your body, and they are connected by tubes called lymph vessels. These vessels are sort of like veins, but they're filled with a fluid called lymph instead of blood.

Your lymph nodes have special white blood cells called **lymphocytes** inside. Lymphocytes make the antibodies that help you fight germs. The antibodies may not keep you from getting sick from germs the first time they get in your body, but they will help you feel less crummy if that germ comes back. This is how many vaccines work!

SUNSCREEN TEST

It's important to protect your skin when you're in the sun. Let's test how well different sunscreens work!

What You Need:

SCISSORS
BLACK CONSTRUCTION PAPER
NON-SUNSCREEN LOTION
TWO OR MORE SUNSCREEN LOTIONS, EACH WITH A DIFFERENT SPF LEVEL
PENCIL
COINS
SUNLIGHT

1. Using scissors, cut the black construction paper into three or more squares. You'll need as many squares as you have lotions.

2. Put some regular (non-sunscreen) lotion on one square of paper. Set it aside.

3. Put a different SPF sunscreen on each of the other squares. Label them with the pencil.

4. Place the squares outside in direct sunlight. Place coins on the corners so they don't blow away.

5. Leave the squares out for a few hours. The longer they're out, the better the results.

6. Compare the squares. The square that stayed the darkest was the most protected. Which lotion was on that paper?

CHAPTER THREE

HOW YOUR BODY MOVES

You don't think about it when you walk, climb, or run, but many different body parts have to work together to allow you to do these things. Your skeletal system is what gives your body shape. It also provides places for muscles to attach.

Muscles make up the muscular system. They attach to your bones and make your skeleton move. Muscles also support your body and help some organs do their jobs.

Finally, your body has **joints** in places that need to bend or turn. They let you move in different directions and are the reason you can dance, draw, or even talk! Ready to learn how your body moves? You'll need all the parts we've just talked about to turn the page.

Your Skeleton

Without your skeleton, you'd be a mushy pile with no shape. Adult human skeletons have 206 bones. Human babies are born with about 300! This is because some bones come together as the baby grows.

The spine is at the center of it all. It helps you stand up tall. It's made of smaller bones called vertebrae (ver-ta-bray). Your ribs are attached to the vertebrae.

Your body has big bones and small bones. Your arms have three big bones each: the humerus, radius, and ulna. Each of your legs has two: the femur and tibia. Your head is also a major bone. It is called the skull.

Where do you think small bones are found? They are in your hands and feet—and even your ears! In fact, the smallest bones in your body are inside your ears. The three bones found there are each smaller than a grain of rice.

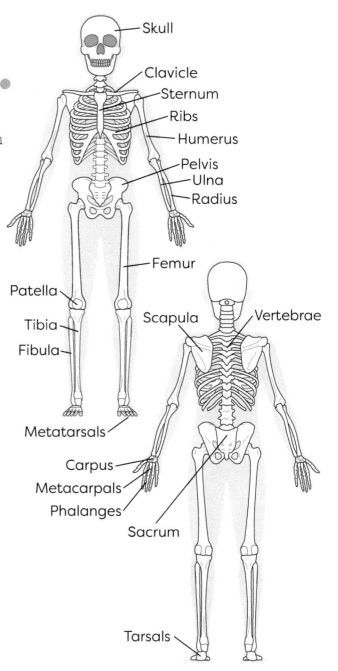

Skull
Clavicle
Sternum
Ribs
Humerus
Pelvis
Ulna
Radius
Femur
Patella
Tibia
Fibula
Metatarsals
Scapula
Vertebrae
Carpus
Metacarpals
Phalanges
Sacrum
Tarsals

Your skeleton is held together with connective tissues called tendons, ligaments, and cartilage. These soft tissues attach bones to one another, as well as to muscles and joints.

Bones are hard and cannot bend; that is where your joints come in. You'll learn about the six types of joints later in this chapter.

Types of Bones

Bones come in all shapes and sizes. Here are the major types of bones:

- **Long bones** are the strongest. They help you move and support your body. The bones in your arms, legs, and your hands and feet (even though those are little!) are all examples of long bones. The longest bone in the body is the femur, which is inside your thigh.

- **Short bones** are shaped like cubes. They are made mostly of spongy bone, which has lots of tiny holes that let blood vessels through them. Your wrist is a collection of short bones, called carpal bones.

- **Tarsal bones** form the middle part of your feet and your heels. They help you move your ankles.

- **Flat bones** are places for muscles to attach. They also protect the soft organs inside them. The skull, pelvis, rib cage, and sternum are flat bones.

- **Sesamoid bones** actually form *inside* of tendons, one of the types of connective tissue. (That's pretty unusual!) Your kneecap bone is a great example. They're called sesamoid bones because most of them are small like a sesame seed.

- **Irregular bones** aren't long, short, tarsal, or flat. They have unique shapes and functions. Vertebrae, the sacrum (say-crum; your tailbone), and most of the bones in the skull are irregular. So is your hyoid. It's a bone in the throat—the only bone not attached to any other bones!

Bones are not solid all the way through. They look like a sponge inside. Blood cells are made in the center of most bones in a place called the bone marrow.

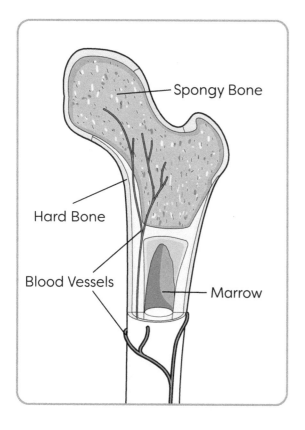

Spongy Bone

Hard Bone

Blood Vessels

Marrow

How You Bend and Twist

Joints are places where two or more bones meet. Without them, you wouldn't be able to turn your head, throw a ball, or walk. Let's check out the six different kinds of joints that help you move.

- **Ball and socket joints** let a body part move in many different directions—like your hips and shoulders.

- **Condyloid joints** help bones move both side to side and up and down—like in your wrist and fingers.

- **Gliding joints** are where two or more mostly flat bones slide across one another—like in your spine and ankles.

- **Hinge joints** move in one direction—like your elbows and knees.

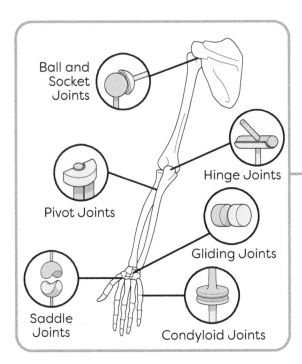

Ball and Socket Joints

Pivot Joints

Hinge Joints

Gliding Joints

Saddle Joints

Condyloid Joints

- **Pivot joints** let parts of your body rotate—like your neck.

- **Saddle joints** can move in more directions than any other joint: side to side, up and down, and in circles. Your thumb has a saddle joint.

It would be easy to wear your bones out from moving your joints all the time. That's why the ends of bones in a joint are covered in cartilage. Cartilage

is a slippery material that lets bones move smoothly against one another. It is one of your body's connective tissues.

Meet Your Muscles

Muscles are made of bundles of muscle cells that work together to do their jobs. They come in many different shapes and sizes, depending on what they do.

SKELETAL MUSCLE

Skeletal muscles are attached to your skeleton with strong bands called tendons. These muscles are what make your body move. They are voluntary muscles. This means that you need to think about moving them to get them to move.

CARDIAC MUSCLE

Your heart is a muscle. It is made out of cardiac muscle cells. They are found only in your heart and nowhere else. This type of muscle is very strong. It is an involuntary muscle, which means that you don't have to think about it for it to do its job.

SMOOTH MUSCLE

Smooth muscle is also an involuntary muscle. It is found in places like your bladder, arteries and veins, stomach, and intestines. The muscles that squeeze food through your digestive system and make your hairs stand up when you are cold are smooth muscles.

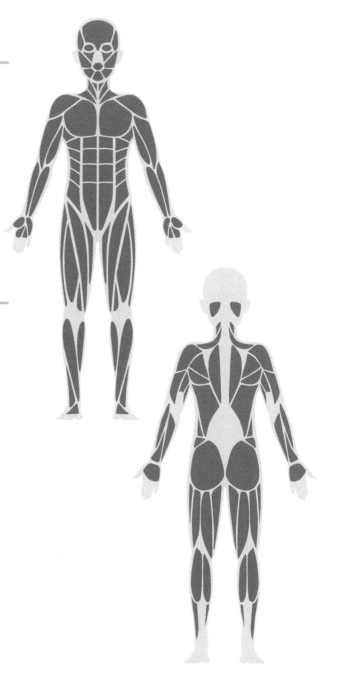

LEND A HAND

Did you know that your hand is made up of 27 bones? Your wrist has eight carpal bones. Your palm is formed by five metacarpal bones—one for each finger. Your fingers each have three phalange bones and your thumb has two.

How do you bend your fingers? With flexor tendons! These tendons are on the palm side of your fingers. They let you bend your fingers by working like a pulley system. Think of how you open and close window blinds. When you pull the string, the blinds go up or down, or side to side. Your flexor tendon is like the string. When the tendon is "pulled," it contracts, or gets shorter. This makes the finger bend. The flexor tendon can't straighten your finger, though. To do that, a tendon on the back of your finger needs to contract. This pulls the finger straight.

WHAT'S SO FUNNY?

Ow! Hitting your funny bone isn't so funny! Your elbow is actually the end of your humerus bone. The painful tingling feeling comes from hitting the ulnar nerve. It is attached to the ulna and humerus bones at the elbow joint.

X-RAY VISION

An X-ray is a special picture that lets doctors see your bones. They use a light box to see the X-ray. Make a light box and look at X-rays at home!

What You Need:

X-RAY IMAGES FROM THE INTERNET
PAPER AND PRINTER
OVERHEAD TRANSPARENCY SHEETS
STRING LIGHTS
LARGE PLASTIC CONTAINER WITH A CLEAR LID
A DARK AREA TO PUT THE BOX

1. Print the X-ray images from the Internet onto plain paper. Ask an adult for help with this.

2. Copy the X-rays onto the overhead transparency sheets. Ask an adult for help with this.

3. Put the string lights into the container and put the lid on. Make sure the plug is outside the box.

4. Find a dark room and plug in the lights.

5. Set the X-ray transparencies on top of the glowing container and check them out!

Safety tip: Make sure to unplug the lights after viewing. They shouldn't be lit while in the plastic container for too long!

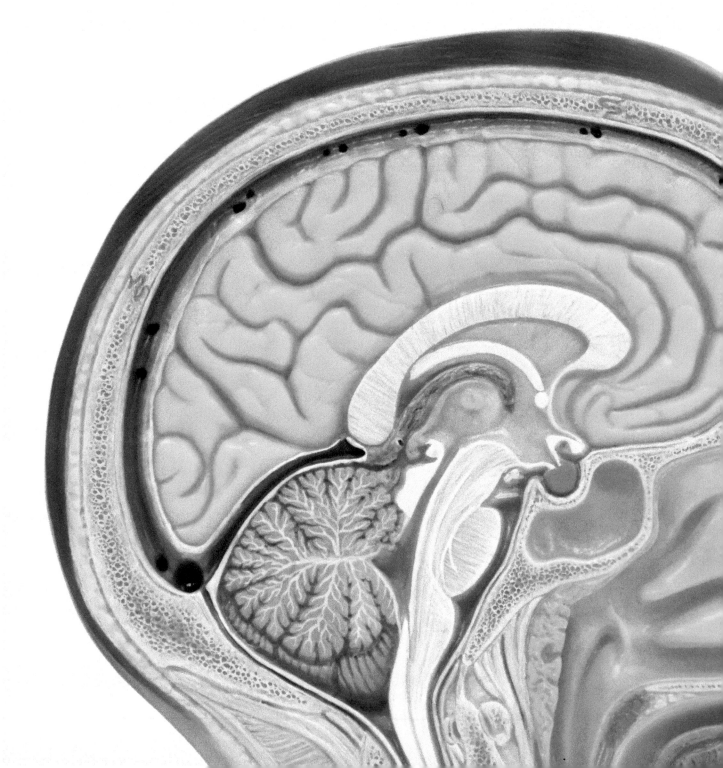

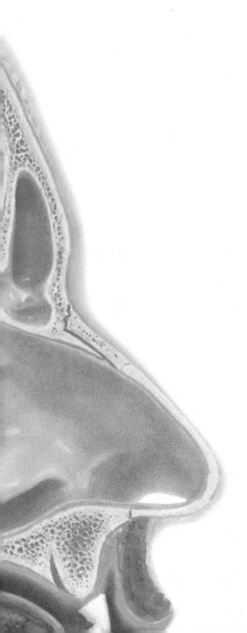

CHAPTER FOUR

MAKING SENSE

No matter what you are doing, your body is always getting messages from the environment. Your nervous system collects information from your sense organs: your nose, mouth, ears, skin, and eyes. All these organs send information to your brain. Your brain takes these messages and works to figure out what they mean. Once your body knows what's happening on the outside, it can learn how to respond on the inside to keep itself in homeostasis, stay comfortable, and avoid danger.

The Nervous System

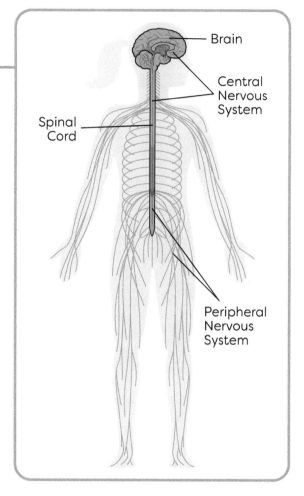

Your nervous system has two main parts: the central nervous system and the peripheral nervous system. Think of this system as a road map with highways and roads that lead to and from your brain. But, instead of roads, information moves around your body using **nerves**, a type of cell.

Your central nervous system includes your brain and spinal cord. It's called "central" because it's in the center of the body. The spinal cord goes from your brain all the way down your back. (It is very important, so it is protected by your vertebrae.) The spinal cord is like a long wire that carries messages to and from the rest of your body! The central nervous system gets messages from the nerves throughout your body, decides how to respond to them, and sends directions back out. It also controls your thoughts and body movements.

The peripheral nervous system is all the nerves in your body—from your head to your feet. It sends information to the central nervous system and then does whatever the brain tells it to do in response.

Meet Your Brain

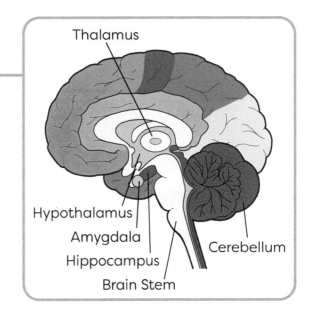

The brain is one of your five vital organs. That means you can't live without it. It controls everything your body does, helps you make sense of the world around you, and stores your memories. More than half of your amazing brain is made up of fat. It is fragile, but your skull does a fantastic job of protecting it.

The outside of the brain is called the cerebrum (suh-ree-brum). It is a pinkish gray color and full of wrinkles. It has four parts, or lobes: the frontal, parietal, temporal, and occipital lobes. The cerebrum controls things like speech, sight, hearing, movement, and problem-solving.

Inside your brain you will find the thalamus, hypothalamus, amygdala, brain stem, and hippocampus. They each control something different:

- The **thalamus** helps make sense of your senses.

- The **hypothalamus** controls your temperature, sleep, and hunger.

- When you are feeling emotional, your **amygdala** is in charge.

- Memories are kept in the **hippocampus**.

- Your **brain stem** controls things like heart rate, breathing, and sneezing.

Another part, the cerebellum (ser-uh-bell-um), looks like a ball of spaghetti at the back of your brain. It helps you keep your balance and helps control the way you move. Whenever you are walking, dancing, playing the piano, or kicking a ball, you are using your cerebellum.

Eyes

Eyes may be small, but they have a big job to do! They translate light into pictures for the brain. The cornea is the clear part that covers your eye and focuses light so the pictures are clear. The pupil is the dark center of your eye. It controls how much light gets in. The colored part, called the iris, makes the pupil get bigger or smaller, depending on how much light is needed to see. A lens behind the pupil focuses light onto the retina at the back of your eye. The retina sends these light messages to the brain. Then the brain tells you what it sees!

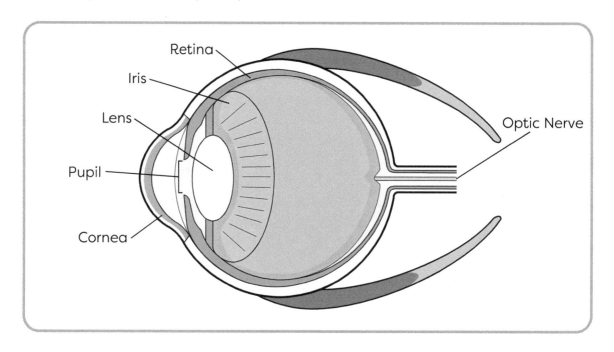

Retina
Iris
Lens
Pupil
Cornea
Optic Nerve

Ears

Ears let you hear sounds, and they have three main parts. The *outer ear* is the part that you can see. It catches sound waves and sends them to your eardrum. The eardrum is a thin piece of skin that moves when sound waves hit it. It's called a "drum" because it acts a lot like the musical instrument does!

The *middle ear* takes the sound's vibrations to the *inner ear*. The cochlea (ko-klee-uh) in the inner ear sends the vibrations to your brain through nerves, and your brain tells you what it hears!

Did you know ears also help you stay balanced? The inner ear has semicircular canals, which have fluid inside and are what help you keep your balance.

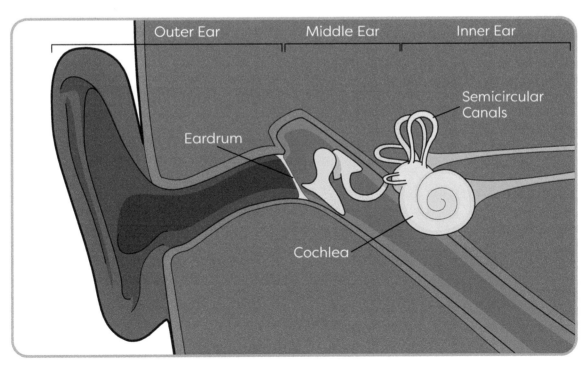

Outer Ear | Middle Ear | Inner Ear

Semicircular Canals

Eardrum

Cochlea

Nose

Your nose is part of your respiratory system. The part you can grab is made of rubbery cartilage. When you breathe in, air enters your nostrils. Nose hair and mucus trap dust and pathogens so they can't get into your body or lungs. Then the air moves into your sinus cavity—the inside part of your nose that makes the mucus. The air is warmed up, moistened, and sent to your lungs.

Your nose has another important skill on top of breathing: it can smell. Your body's cells react with chemicals in the air to form smells. Everything from cookies in the oven to the spray from a skunk releases chemicals. Your nose senses those chemicals and sends the information to your brain. Then your brain tells you what it is smelling.

Did you know that your nose also helps you taste things? When you chew food, it releases more chemicals for your nose to pick up. Your nose sends

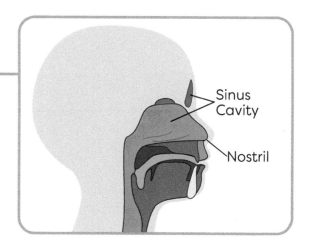

Sinus Cavity

Nostril

this information to your brain and you taste what you are eating! This is why food doesn't taste like much when you have a stuffy nose.

WHAT'S A BOOGER?

Booger is another word for dried mucus. Mucus is made in your nose to trap dirt and germs. It grabs the dirt and germs, dries up, and turns into boogers! The best way to get rid of boogers is to blow them into a tissue. Picking your nose can damage the mucous membranes and let more dirt and germs in.

Mouth

You use your mouth to breathe, eat, and speak.

You chew food with teeth, which are part of the skeletal system. But your teeth would have a hard time without your tongue! Nerves in your tongue can sense how soft or hard your food is, and your brain knows to move tougher food to the back of your mouth so the strong molar teeth can grind it. Your tongue is also a strong muscle that lets you taste your food and swallow it. It can measure five different tastes: salty, sweet, spicy, sour, and savory. (Other flavors like vanilla, pear, or fish are actually sensed by your nose!)

Your tongue also works with your vocal cords to help you form words. Your vocal cords are deep in your throat. They have three very important jobs: They vibrate to make noise when

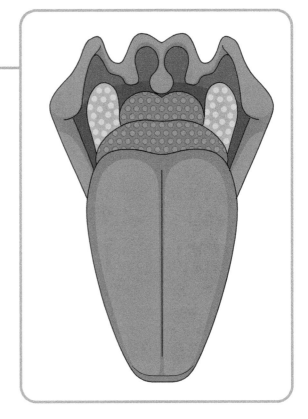

you sing or talk. They help keep things that don't belong out of your breathing tube. And they control the air that flows into your lungs.

RIGHT BRAIN VS. LEFT BRAIN

The cerebrum has two halves: the right brain and the left brain. Each half controls the opposite side of the body. This means the right side of your brain is in charge of the left side of your body, while the left side of your brain controls the right side of your body.

What does each half do? The right brain is active when you are being creative. It's active when you do things like write a story, use your imagination, feel emotions, or express yourself by gesturing or making faces without even meaning to. The left side is active during organized activities. It's active when you do things like give a speech, do math, practice science, make plans, or think about what's around you.

Both sides of the brain work together to receive information from your surroundings and make sense of it.

GLAND-TASTIC

The endocrine system makes **hormones**. Hormones are chemical signals that control the ways your body works.

Some hormones let you know when you feel hungry and some make you feel sleepy when it's time for bed. Other hormones help your body grow and develop. There is even a hormone that can give you a burst of energy when you are in danger.

Hormones are made inside small organs called glands. They are found throughout your body. Some are in your brain (pituitary gland, hypothalamus, and pineal). There is one in your neck (thyroid), chest (thymus), and abdomen (pancreas), and two above your kidneys (adrenal). You also have endocrine glands in your testes if you are a boy, and in your ovaries if you are a girl. (You'll learn more about these body parts in chapter 7.)

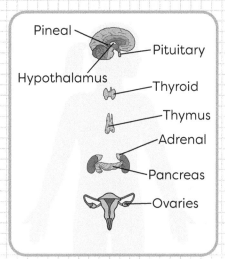

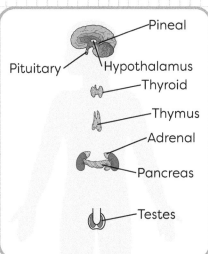

TASTE TEST

You've learned that your sense of smell plays a big role in how you taste things. Let's find out if it can change the way your food tastes!

What You Need:

Choose five (or more) different foods from this list—or make your own list!

APPLESAUCE
BANANA
BLUEBERRIES
HAM
ICE CREAM
JELLY
ORANGE JUICE
PEANUT BUTTER
PICKLE
POTATO CHIPS
SOUR CANDY
STRAWBERRIES

1. Taste each food.

2. Then, pinch your nose shut while you taste each one again.

3. How did pinching your nose change how the food tasted? Did the taste of all the foods change? Could you tell what you were eating?

4. Try this experiment with a partner. Close your eyes, pinch your nose, and have your partner put a piece of food in your mouth. Can you tell what it is?

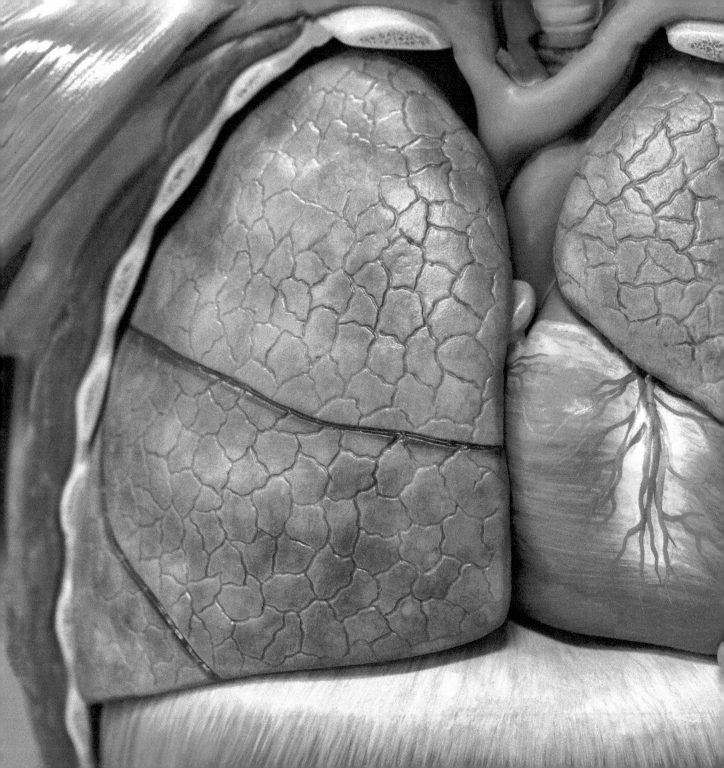

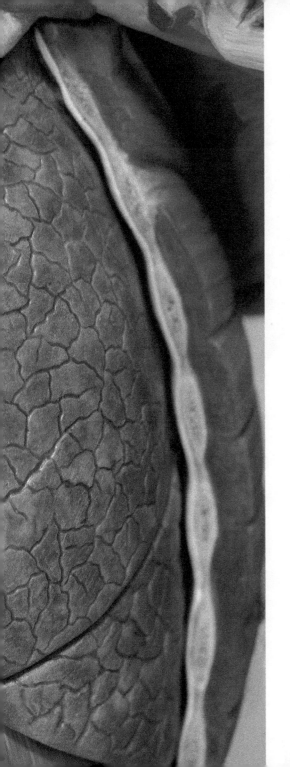

CHAPTER FIVE

BREATHING TO THE BEAT

Two systems that work very closely together are the circulatory and respiratory systems. They split the job of getting oxygen and nutrients to every part of your body.

Let's start with your circulatory system. This system makes blood flow through your lungs. The blood picks up oxygen from your lungs, and then it goes to the digestive system to pick up nutrients from food. Finally, it brings those things to every one of your cells. Your heart is the center of this system.

Heart

Put your hand on your chest. Do you feel thumping? That's your heart! Your heart is a muscle that pumps blood through your entire body—and never stops. The blood moves inside tubes called veins and arteries. These are also called blood vessels. An adult has more than 100,000 miles of these blood vessels—enough to wrap around Earth more than four times!

Your heart has four chambers, or spaces, that blood travels through. The atria are the two upper chambers. The ventricles are the two lower chambers. These four chambers help your blood pick up oxygen.

First, blood without oxygen goes into one of the upper chambers, called the right atrium. It goes through a very large vein called the vena cava. Then, the blood is pumped into one of the lower chambers, called the right ventricle. The right ventricle sends blood

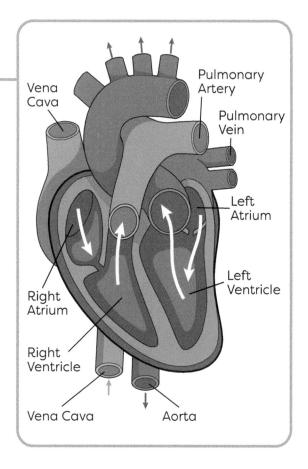

through arteries to the lungs, where it picks up oxygen. The oxygenated blood comes back through the left atrium and flows into the left ventricle. This is the thickest chamber, because its job is to pump that blood to your *entire* body!

BLOOD

Everyone knows what blood is, but what exactly does it do? Blood is what carries important nutrients, hormones, and oxygen throughout your body. It also takes waste away and helps fight infections.

More than half of blood is plasma (plaz-muh)—the liquid part that is mostly water. Hormones, nutrients, and proteins are part of the plasma. Red blood cells, white blood cells, and platelets float in the plasma. Red blood cells pick up oxygen from the lungs and deliver it to the body. White blood cells help the body fight germs, disease, and infections. Platelets stop your cuts from bleeding by sticking together to make a clot or scab.

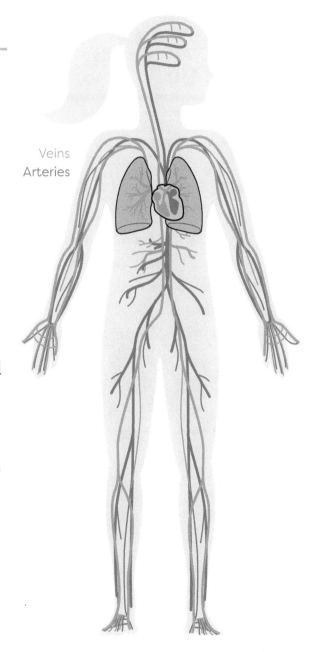

Veins
Arteries

Breathe In, Breathe Out

The circulatory system would be useless without the respiratory system. Its job is to bring in oxygen so the red blood cells can pick it up—and get rid of the waste gas called carbon dioxide. Your nose, mouth, windpipe (or breathing tube), and lungs are all part of the respiratory system.

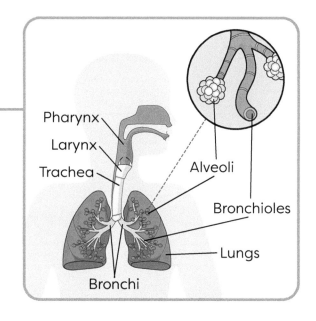

Pharynx

Larynx

Trachea

Alveoli

Bronchioles

Lungs

Bronchi

When you take a breath, air enters the nose and mouth. It goes down your throat and into your windpipe—which leads to your two lungs. The air moves through small branches called bronchi (bronk-eye). Then it moves through the bronchioles, which look like smaller tree branches. Finally, the air reaches the alveoli (al-vee-o-lie). These are tiny sacs that take oxygen from the air and remove carbon dioxide from the blood—and you can have up to 600 million of them!

Carbon dioxide leaves your body when you breathe out. The diaphragm (die-a-fram) is a flat muscle below the lungs. It moves down to fill your lungs and pushes up to empty them. Try this: Put one hand just above your belly button. Take a deep breath in, and then breathe out. Does it feel like your stomach is getting bigger and smaller as your breathe? That's your diaphragm working!

Lungs

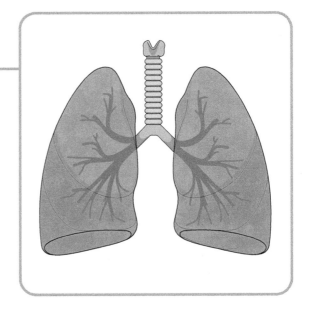

The lungs are the stars of your respiratory system. You have two of them and they take up a lot more space than you may think—from just under your shoulders down to your belly button! The left lung is slightly smaller and has a space for your heart. Healthy lungs are pink and look a bit like giant sponges. They are protected by the rib cage.

The lungs' main job is to take in air for you to breathe. They are also what allows you to talk. The air that you are exhaling from your lungs is what makes your vocal cords vibrate to make sound. Sometimes dirt or food makes it into your windpipe. Your body gets rid of it by coughing—which is when your lungs quickly force air out your mouth.

TAKE YOUR PULSE

Have you ever felt your pulse? When you feel your pulse, you're feeling the rush of blood moving through your blood vessels as your heart beats! You can feel your pulse in a couple of different places. If you place your pointer and middle finger together where the corner of your jaw meets your neck you will feel the pulse in your neck. You can also feel it by gently laying those same two fingers over the thumb-side of your inner wrist.

To take your pulse, set a timer for 30 seconds and count the number of beats you feel during that time. Multiply that number by 2 and you will get your heart rate per minute! Try doing 25 jumping jacks and taking your pulse again. How has it changed?

BABY BEATS

Did you know that your heart started beating before you were born? Doctors used something called an ultrasound machine to see what babies look like and hear their heartbeat from outside the mom's belly.

WHAT'S A BLOOD TYPE?

Everyone has blood. But is everyone's blood the same? Not quite. There are four different blood types: A, B, AB, or O blood. Each of these types can be positive or negative. If you have type A blood, that means you have something called A **antigens**. If you have type B blood, you have B antigens. AB type blood has both A and B antigens. O blood has no antigens at all. Do you know your blood type?

Adults can donate blood to hospitals for people who are sick or having surgery. People that have the same blood type can donate blood to one another. People with O blood have a special skill. They can donate to a person with any blood type!

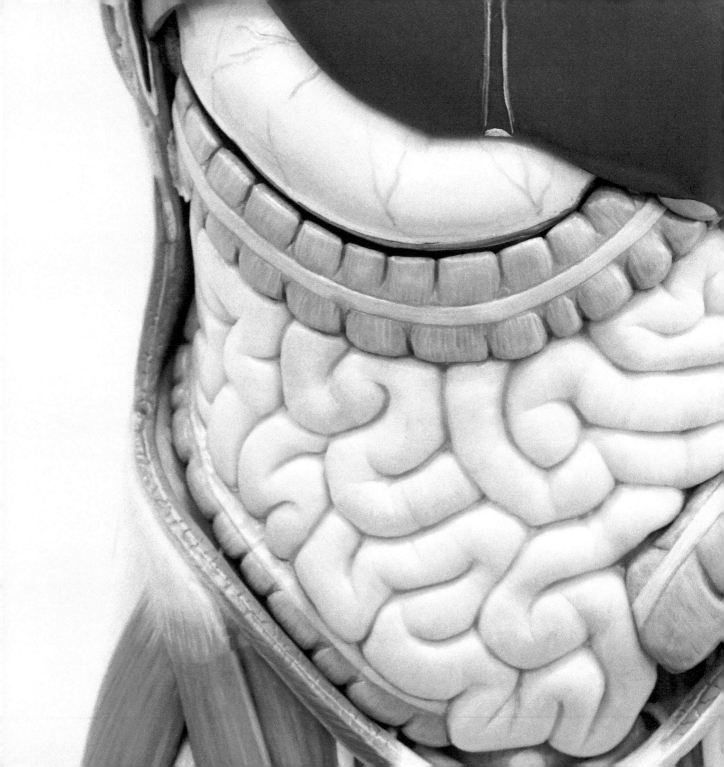

CHAPTER SIX

LET'S EAT!

Everyone knows you need to eat to live, but where does the food go after you swallow it? Turning food into something the body can use is the digestive system's job! **Digestion** is the process of eating food, breaking it down, taking the nutrients out, and getting rid of what's left as waste.

Food travels from your mouth to your esophagus, stomach, small intestine, large intestine, and finally to the colon and rectum. There are helpful bacteria in your digestive system called gut bacteria that help you break down the food that you eat. Without these bacteria, food would sit in your system for way too long! Your digestive system is really great at making sure your body only keeps the stuff it needs and gets rid of anything it doesn't.

Break It Down

Digestion begins in your mouth. Your teeth chew food and mash it into small pieces. Then your saliva (or spit) gets to work. It has chemicals called **enzymes** that start breaking down the food into materials your body can use. Once things are nice and mushy, you can swallow food. Then it enters your esophagus (es-ah-fuh-gus).

The esophagus is a hollow, muscular tube that brings food to your stomach by contracting, or squeezing, the muscles in waves. If those muscles don't work well, food and drinks can have a hard time getting to your stomach.

Into the Stomach

Welcome to your stomach—the bag-shaped organ located under your rib cage. Just like your esophagus, your stomach uses muscles to move the food around and break it up. The stomach turns the food into a soupy mix called chyme (kime). The chyme is easier for the intestines to handle during the next step of digestion.

Your stomach also dissolves food using acid. It makes a special stomach acid called *acidic gastric juice* just for this job. This process gets the food ready to release its nutrients. Stomach acid has to be very strong to do the job it does. So, why doesn't it digest your stomach? The stomach has a layer of mucus that protects it!

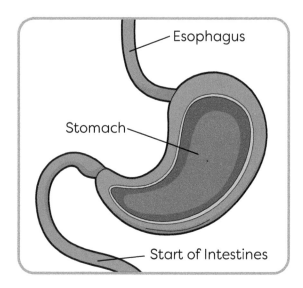

Esophagus

Stomach

Start of Intestines

I FEEL SICK

Have you ever eaten something that made you feel icky? You may have even thrown up. You throw up when your brain decides that something you ate or drank is a danger to your body. That could be anything from spoiled food to a pathogen.

Throwing up is a way your body protects itself. Your brain tells your stomach muscles to squeeze hard. Those muscles bring the food—usually mixed with stomach acid—back up your esophagus and out your mouth. It is pretty unpleasant, but the next time it happens, remember your body is doing it for your own good! You might also throw up when you are stressed or are swaying a lot (like in the car or on a boat).

The Liver and Friends

Your liver is your largest internal organ. It sits under your rib cage and on top of your stomach, right kidney, and intestines. Blood leaves the stomach and intestines and goes through the liver.

The liver has several jobs. One is to clean your blood by removing toxins and waste. Another is to break down fats and proteins so the body can use them. It also stores vitamins and minerals that it releases into your blood when needed. Finally, your liver makes something called bile that is stored under the liver in the gallbladder. Bile is released into the small intestine to help break down fats into fatty acids that can be used by the body.

Behind the stomach is another organ, called the pancreas (pan-kree-us). Your pancreas makes enzymes that help the liver with digestion and help your intestines absorb nutrients from your food. Your pancreas

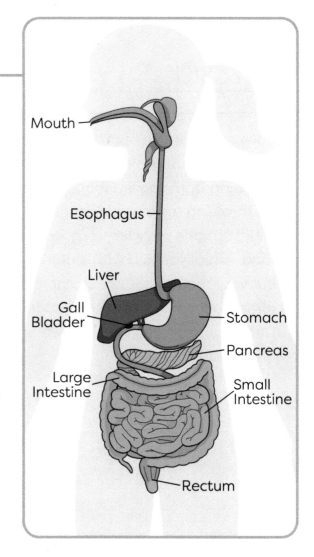

also makes hormones that ensure you have the right levels of sugar in your blood.

Into the Intestines

The small and large intestines are the next stop in digestion. Food moves from the stomach to the small intestines first.

As food moves through the small intestine, several things happen. The chyme continues to get crushed. Different enzymes break it down even further, and the food's vitamins and nutrients are absorbed into the blood.

Then, the chyme arrives at the large intestine, or colon (kole-un). At this point, it's time to package up the waste and send it out of the body. The large intestine absorbs as much water as it can from the chyme as it's pushed through. The body can use that water. Once the material gets to the rectum, it's solid and much drier. It is now feces, or poop! The rectum stores the feces until you are ready to go to the bathroom and get rid of it. You're done digesting!

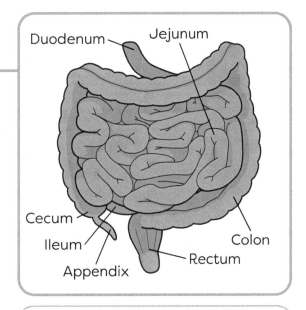

THE APPENDIX

The appendix is a small tube located where your small and large intestine meet. It's confusing to doctors, because they're not quite sure what it does. It's a little organ that can cause BIG problems if it gets infected. This kind of infection is called appendicitis (uh-pen-dis-i-tis). It often means the appendix needs to be removed. Good thing it is one of the only organs you can live without!

Where Does Pee Come From?

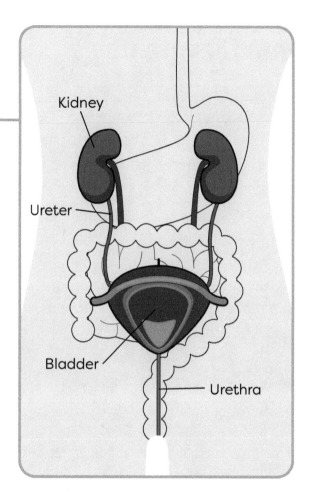

You've just learned how food is digested and where that waste goes when your body is done with it. But where does other waste go? Non-food waste builds up in different parts of the body, including the blood. The urinary system helps you get rid of this waste. The kidneys and bladder are where the action happens.

Your two kidneys are amazing filters that clean your blood and remove waste and extra water. As the kidneys do their job, they make urine, which is liquid waste. The urine travels to the bladder down thin spaghetti-like tubes called ureters. The bladder is like an empty balloon. It can expand to hold up to two cups of urine in an adult so you only need to pee a few times a day instead of all the time! Urine leaves your body through a tube called the urethra (yer-eeth-ruh).

IT'S A GAS!

Sometimes you swallow too much air while you are eating, especially if you are eating fast. This can feel uncomfortable. Your body makes you feel better by burping! How does this happen? When there is too much air in your stomach, it gets forced back up through the esophagus and becomes a burp. The sound comes from the pressure of the air going through a muscular ring in the esophagus that opens to let food in and then closes to keep it in.

What about farts? They can also be caused by swallowing too much air, or they can happen when food is hard to digest. Gases are released by certain foods as they are digested by your gut bacteria. When the gas builds up and needs to come out, you fart. It's super normal and healthy to fart many times a day!

DIGEST THIS!

Let's make a model stomach at home!

What You Need:

SLICE OF BREAD
RESEALABLE BAG
2 TO 3 TABLESPOONS OF WATER

1. Tear the bread into bite-size pieces. (Consider this the "chewing" part of digestion.)

2. Put the pieces of bread and 2 to 3 tablespoons of water inside the resealable bag. Seal the bag.

3. Squeeze the bag with your hands to mimic how your stomach breaks down food. You will notice that the food inside the bag gets squished up and soupy—just like food does inside your stomach.

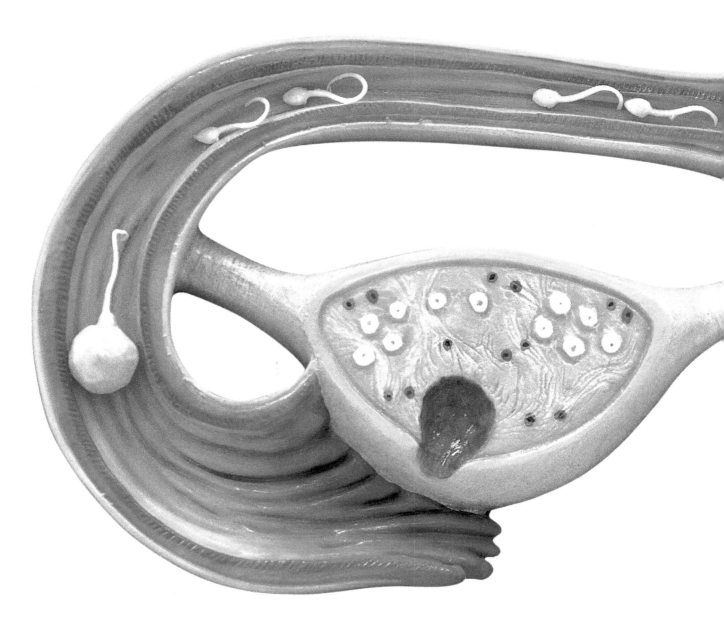

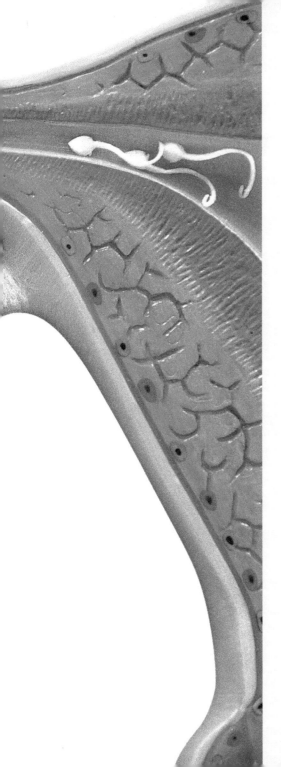

CHAPTER SEVEN

GROW UP

Reproduction is how living things make more living things—in our case, a new human. The reproductive system is the only system that has different parts in female and male bodies.

The cells in this system that create a baby are called sex cells. In women, these are eggs. In men, these are sperm. Each sex cell has only half the information, called **genes**, that a new baby needs to grow. It takes one egg and one sperm to make a new human. When these two cells come together, they grow into a baby!

Female Reproductive Organs

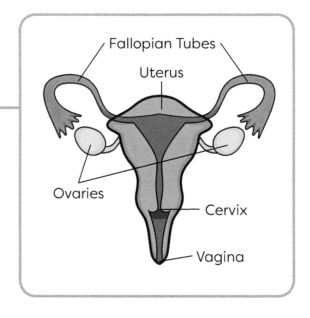

The female reproductive system is made up of mostly internal parts. The uterus (yoo-ter-us), also called the womb, is on the inside. This is where babies grow inside of mothers. Also inside are two ovaries. They store the woman's eggs (her sex cells). Fallopian tubes connect the uterus to the ovaries.

The cervix is the bottom part of the uterus. It leads to the vagina, which is a muscular tube that runs to the outside of the body. Breasts are part of the female reproductive system, too. In adult women, they make milk for a baby when it is born.

When kids get older, both boys and girls go through something called **puberty**. During puberty, their bodies change. When girls go through puberty, they start something called **menstruation**. Menstruation, or a period, happens every month when an egg is released into the uterus. If the egg isn't fertilized by a male sex cell, the uterus gets rid of the egg. The egg and the lining of the uterus come out of the body. (We'll read more about fertilization on page 62.)

Male Reproductive Organs

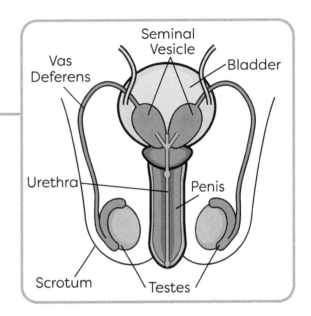

The male reproductive system has internal and external organs. Sperm cells (male sex cells) are made and stored inside the testes. Testes are in the scrotum on the outside of the body. The scrotum protects the testes and keeps them at the right temperature for sperm to survive. If they are too hot or too cold, the sperm will die.

There are glands inside a man's body, like the prostate gland, that make fluids that feed the sperm and make it easier for them to move. Sperm move through a tube called the vas deferens and into the urethra. The urethra in males is inside the penis. Sperm move through the urethra and out the penis.

Reproduction

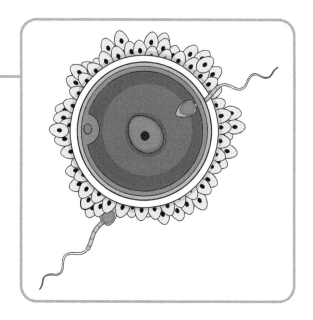

What do you need to make a baby? One egg and one sperm. When these cells come together, it is called **fertilization**. In humans, fertilization happens when a sperm cell joins with an egg cell inside the uterus. It takes about nine months for a baby to develop enough to live outside the uterus! So many things happen during that time.

Six weeks after fertilization, the baby's organs start to grow and its heart begins to beat. After two months, the baby's brain, spinal cord, and face form. After three months, ears, hands, arms, fingers, feet, and nails form. After four months, the baby's eyes can move, and the baby begins to hear. Around five months, the baby starts to grow hair and form fingerprints. After six months, they can respond to sound and open their eyes. The baby keeps growing and developing until the ninth month. By this time, things are getting pretty cramped in the uterus. It's time to be born!

When it's time to be born, the baby leaves the uterus and comes out of the body through the vagina. Sometimes a doctor has to take the baby directly out of the uterus. Either way it happens, a new baby has come into the world!

MORE TO DISCOVER

RECOMMENDED BOOKS

FACTIVITY: JOURNEY AROUND AND INSIDE YOUR AMAZING BODY BY PARRAGON BOOKS

HUMAN BODY ACTIVITY BOOK FOR KIDS BY KATIE STOKES, MEd, PhD

THE MAGIC SCHOOL BUS PRESENTS: THE HUMAN BODY BY DAN GREEN AND CAROLYN BRACKEN

PEEKING UNDER YOUR SKIN (WHAT'S BENEATH) BY KAREN LATCHANA KENNEY AND STEVEN WOOD

RECOMMENDED WEBSITES

SCHOLASTIC'S STUDY JAMS!

StudyJams.Scholastic.com/studyjams/jams/science/human-body/human-body.htm

WONDEROPOLIS

Wonderopolis.org/wonders?q=human+body

RECOMMENDED APPS

THE HUMAN BODY BY TINYBOP

GLOSSARY

ADAPTIVE RESPONSE (UH-DAP-TIV REE-SPONS): When the immune system makes antibodies to fight specific germs and learns how to fight them in the future

ANATOMY (UH-NAT-OH-MEE): The body parts of an organism and the study of those parts

ANTIBODY (AN-TEE-BOD-EE): A special protein in the blood that sticks to a specific germ and alerts the immune system to attack it

ANTIGEN (AN-TI-JEN): The structure on a cell that an antibody can stick to and alert the immune system

BLOOD VESSELS: Small tubes in the body through which blood flows to reach all the different parts

CELL (SELL): The smallest part of any body that makes up all the other tissues and organs

CONNECTIVE TISSUES: Soft tissues that attach bones, muscles, and joints to one another and hold organs in place. These tissues are called tendons, ligaments, and cartilage

DIGESTION (DI-JEST-CHUN): The process of turning food into nutrients the body can use

DNA: The abbreviation for *deoxyribonucleic acid* (de-oxee-rye-bow-new-clay-ick as-sid), which are the instructions found in all cells that control how a body grows and looks

ENZYME (EN-ZIME): A chemical in the human body that is able to break down a substance into a new substance the body can use

FERTILIZATION (FUR-TILL-I-ZAY-SHUN): When a sperm cell and egg cell come together

GENE (JEEN): The information in DNA that comes from both parents that decides how an organism looks and acts

GLANDS: A group of cells that make different substances in the body that are released into the bloodstream

HOMEOSTASIS (HO-MEE-OH-STAY-SIS): In the human body, the ability to keep things like temperature and the amount of water in the tissues in balance

HORMONE (HOR-MOAN): Chemicals that are made in the body that tell it to do certain things, like break down food or control the amount of sugar in the blood

IMMUNITY (IM-MEWN-IT-EE): The ability to fight off pathogens that were in the body once before with antibodies

INNATE RESPONSE (IN-NATE REE-SPONS): The body's first attempts to keep germs out of the body (with skin and/or hair) and fight them if they get in (with blood chemicals and special white cells)

JOINT: The point where two bones connect to one another

LYMPHOCYTE (LIM-FO-SITE): A small white blood cell in the lymphatic system that helps fight pathogens

LYMPH NODES (LIMF NODES): Small, bean-shaped structures in the body's immune system that filter out germs and help fight infection

MENSTRUATION (MEN-STREW-AY-SHUN): The process of the uterus shedding its lining once a month if fertilization doesn't happen; also called a period

MUSCLES: The tissues that make up the muscular system and control all of the body's movement

NERVES: Fibers that send impulses to and from the brain and the rest of the body

ORGAN (OR-GUN): A collection of different tissues that work together to do a job

ORGAN SYSTEM: A group of organs in a body that work together to complete a task

PATHOGEN (PATH-O-JEN): A microscopic organism that can make you sick, especially a virus or bacterium

PUBERTY (PEW-BER-TEE): The time in a human's life when the body goes through changes to be able to reproduce

REPRODUCTION (REE-PRO-DUCK-SHUN): When an organism makes others of its kind

TISSUE (TISH-EW): A collection of cells that work together to do a certain job

TOXIN (TOCKS-IN): A poison that can make you sick or cause death

INDEX

Throwing up, 51
Tissues, 2, 4–5, 6–7
Tongue, 35

U

Ultrasound machines, 46
Urethra, 54, 61
Urinary system, 6–7, 54
Uterus, 60, 62

V

Vagina, 60
Vas deferens, 61
Vellus hair, 13

X

X-rays, 26

ABOUT THE AUTHOR

Kristie Wagner is currently a middle school science teacher in southeast Wisconsin. She previously taught five years of high school science and has a master of science degree in ecological teaching and learning. In her teaching career, she has designed curriculum for physical science (grades 8, 10), biology (grades 9, 10), advanced biology (grade 12), anatomy and physiology (grade 11), and environmental science (grades 11, 12). Kristie currently works on a climate-change education team creating and reviewing content for the North American Association for Environmental Education, which she has done for the last three years. She lives with her husband and son near a nature preserve. She loves to hike, write in her nature journal, and read. She always finds resources to help her keep learning new things!

CPSIA information can be obtained
at www.ICGtesting.com
Printed in the USA
JSHW012027110722
27922JS00004B/12

9 781648 768637